Freight Forwarder Business Startup

How to Start, Run & Grow a Successful freight Forwarding Business

By

Allen McCarthy

Published by:

www.Valenciapub.com

Valencia Publishing House
P.O. Box 548
Wilmer, Alabama 36587

Cover & Interior designed

By

Alex Lockridge

First Edition

CONTENTS

INTRODUCTION

IF YOU have decided to become a freight forwarder, then you have made a decision to start a lucrative small business within the freight, transportation, logistics and cargo industries. The prospects within the transportation industry are positive, with a growing income and an increasing demand for skilled specialists. Freight forwarders are the go-to individuals for customers to ship products including a variety of transport methods such as air, highway, rail and sea.

This is an industry that in my opinion still in its infancy, with TPP, TAP and many other global trade agreements, the need for such services will grow higher every year.

Another rapid growth I am seeing in this business is from all the Amazon FBA(Fulfilled By Amazon) business owners, most of who buy their merchandise from China. Now Amazon never accept merchandise directly from a foreign country, so each and every piece of merchandise has to come through a freight forwarder/broker. This way the merchandise can get relabeled and shipped to various Amazon warehouses.

If you are thinking about getting into this business, trust me when I say this, there is not a better time than now to get started. Do your research, get educated, get started

However, there are a few steps you need to take to make sure you are starting your business right and keeping it thriving. Let's take a look at this growing business and what you need to know to get started. First, let's consider just what a freight forwarder is.

WHAT IS A FREIGHT FORWARDER

A FREIGHT forwarder is also known as a non-vessel operating common carrier (NVOCC). They are a person or company that organizes shipments for individuals or corporations to get goods from a manufacturer or producer to a final point of distribution whether it is a market or customer.

Freight forwarders contract with multiple carriers in order to move goods. The forwarder doesn't move the goods themselves, but they are experts in the logistics network. They use a variety of shipping methods such as ships, airplanes, trucks and railroads; sometimes using multiple methods for a single shipment.

International freight forwarders are responsible for handling international shipments. This means they have additional knowledge when preparing and processing customs and other documentation or activities related to international shipments.

There are a number of reasons why a company or consumer may choose to hire a freight forwarder rather than internally or personally arranging transport for their goods. Often the biggest reason for this is to get the best rate along with faster shipping for goods. A successful freight forwarder often has strong contacts within the shipping industry and is often aware of shipping options not available to the general public.

A typical event for a freight forwarder starts when they are contacted by a customer. Initially, information is gathered such as the merchandise being shipped if it has to cross international borders and other important issues (such as weight, size, perishable or nonperishable, hazardous or non-hazardous, etc.) regarding the shipment. Based on this information, the forwarder looks at all the shipping options available and gets the package to its destination on time and at a very competitive price.

Based on this it is easy to see how a freight forwarder can be confused with other similar jobs. The two most common jobs that a freight forwarder is often confused with includes freight broker and customs broker. Before we continue to consider freight forwarding, let's take a moment to see how a freight forwarder is different from these two jobs.

DIFFERENCE BETWEEN FREIGHT FORWARDER AND CUSTOMS BROKER

A customs broker acts as an agent of importers/exporters with the goal being the smooth clearance of cargo at customs. Clearing customs is a very technical and highly regulated process, and many importers/exporters prefer to let the experts handle the process.

A customs broker is a company or individual that is licensed to transact customs business on behalf of other companies or individuals. The customs business is limited entirely to activities that involve the transactions of entry and admissibility of merchandise, its classification and valuation, the payment of duties, taxes or other charges of such goods.

Customs broker is a very specialized job, requires a lot of training and various certifications to be a one. The freight brokerage company I started with had 325 employees, but out of those 325, only two were customs brokers. So you can see that every mid to large size freight, and logistics company will employ a limited number of these especially skilled individuals but most smaller freight brokerage companies operate without such custom's broker on board. As most smaller freight brokerage companies deal mostly with moving freight within the country, where there is no need for a customs broker.

HOW TO DISTINGUISH

Freight forwarders act as a shipping agent and see that businesses are following shipping requirements along with export documentations. A customs broker looks after the transactions at the customs part of international trade from the point of entry, to the payment of taxes, duties or charge including any refunds or rebates. When it comes to the areas of operations, both of these jobs are very different.

A freight forwarder will perform the following five duties:

1. Helps businesses to get the best price quotes for shipping goods.

2. Packages and crates merchandise as well as making arrangements at the port.

3. Booking of cargo space.

4. Arranging for a warehouse facility.

5. Reviewing of documents.

A customs broker will perform the following five duties:

1. Provide businesses with landing costs for shipments entering specific countries.

2. Works with freight forwarders to help clear shipments through customs.

3. Keep in touch with regulators.

4. Pay taxes and charges.

5. Classify and value goods according to a country's customs and import/export tax rates and policy.

DIFFERENCE BETWEEN FREIGHT FORWARDER AND FREIGHT BROKERS

While a freight forwarder and broker may appear the same, they are both legally and technically different from each other. A freight broker is similar to other types of brokers, with the primary purpose of bringing together a buyer and seller.

In the case, a freight broker is bringing together a buyer or a shipper of goods and a seller or the carrier of the goods. The broker is responsible for negotiating the terms of the deal and handling the paperwork. A freight broker business has proper industry knowledge and contacts, but can also be run out of a home office.

HOW TO DISTINGUISH

A freight forwarder essentially has the ability to do the nine following things:

1. Storing a client's cargo at a warehouse.

2. Arranging the distribution or forwarding of cargo per instructions from clients.

3. Negotiating freight rates with a shipping line to cover their client's interests.

4. Booking the cargo with the shipping line based on the client's requirement.

5. Prepare bills of lading and associated shipping or negotiating documents.

6. Issuing approved house bill of lading as necessary.

7. Possibly do customs clearance.

8. Possibly be accredited to do customs and port work.

9. Sometimes viewed as an alternative shipping line by clients.

A freight broker essentially has the ability to do the four following things:

1. Arranges the transportation of goods with a carrier on behalf of a shipper, consignee or freight forwarder.

2. Connects cargo owners with shipping lines or the other way around on a commission basis.

3. Outsources all activities involved in the transportation of goods such as transport and insurance.

4. A freight broker doesn't own their own bills of lading as a freight forwarder does.

A freight forwarding operation is typically bigger than a freight brokerage business. As you can tell a freight forwarding company often has to offer warehouse facilities, manage multimode shipping, can own the bill of lading, etc., so it may hard to do for one individual, whereas a freight broker has much less work and responsibility and can be handled by just one person.

Now that we have an understanding of a freight forwarder and what makes them different from other similar positions within the transportation industry let's consider just what it is a freight forwarder does.

WHAT IS FREIGHT FORWARDING BUSINESS

Freight forwarding is a service used by companies that work with international or multi-national import and export processes. While a freight forwarder doesn't actually move the freight, they act as an intermediary between the clients and various transportation services. Sending products between international destinations involves several carriers, requirements, and legalities. Freight forwarding handles all of these logistics on behalf of the client, relieving them of a huge burden and headache.

Freight forwarding guarantees that the goods will reach its proper destination by an agreed upon date and in good condition. Freight forwarding relies on established relationships with all types of carriers from air freighters to trucking companies. Freight forwarding also ensures that the best possible price is negotiated to move goods at the best economic routes while also getting the best speed and reliability for cost.

Freight forwarding services often provide a client with one or more estimates and advisements when necessary. The price will be affected by the origin and destination of the goods to the special requirements involved such as refrigeration or hazardous materials.

If a client accepts the bid of a freight forwarder, then the goods are prepared for shipping. The freight forwarder then assumes responsibility for the goods until they reach their destination.

Freight forwarding is valued by companies and individuals because it handles ancillary services as a part of the international shipping business. For example, it includes insurance and customs documentation and international customs clearance.

A freight forwarding service is a consolidator and makes it simple for a client to move goods. Let's consider a brief history of the freight forwarder.

A BRIEF HISTORY OF THE FREIGHT FORWARDER

The earliest known freight forwarder was Thomas Meadows of London, England who established his Limited Company in 1836. The introduction of reliable rail transportation and steamships created a demand for the freight forwarding industry.

Additional demand was created from increased trade between Europe and North America. Most of the early freight forwarders were London innkeepers who held and re-forwarded personal effects of hotel guests.

The original purpose of the freight forwarder was to arrange for carriage of goods by contracting with various carriers. A forwarder also offered advice on documentation and customs requirements in the destination country. A correspondent agent overseas was responsible for looking after the goods and keeping the freight forwarder informed about matters that could affect the transportation of goods.

Today, the freight forwarder has very similar duties and responsibilities. They can operate either as a domestic carrier or with a corresponding agent overseas.

Within a single business transaction, a freight forwarder can act as a carrier or as an agent of the client or both.

HOW TO BECOME A FREIGHT FORWARDER

I F YOU choose to become a freight forwarder you are going to be working on behalf of importers and exporters; your focus is going to be on securing freight. This is why a freight forwarder is also sometimes referred to as a cargo agent or freight agent.

As a freight forwarder, you need to become an expert in appropriate cargo transportation methods for moving all kinds of cargo. You will also need to become an expert in the process of booking the cargo itself. Your knowledge needs to include the whole spectrum of freight costs: the actual moving, handling, insurance, necessary documentation and all charges involved in freight handling and moving.

This includes international coordination and export papers if needed. Often you'll need more financial resources and credit on hand than actual freight forwarders. There are also specific types of freight forwarders with various requirements that you need to consider.

TYPES OF FREIGHT FORWARDERS

A freight forwarder that works with surface freight such as trucks and railroads and those who work with ocean freight are required to have federal licenses. In addition, ocean freight forwarders need experience in ocean freight. Airfreight freight forwarders don't need special licensing or experience but do need to go through industry training. Let's briefly look at all the types of freight forwarders and what they need.

OCEAN TRANSPORTATION INTERMEDIARIES

In order to get a license as an ocean transportation intermediary, you need to have three years of documented experience with a firm that is licensed as an ocean transportation intermediary in US foreign commerce.

You need to approach the Federal Maritime Commission to file a Form FMC-18 or "Application for License as an Ocean Transportation Intermediary." The fee as of July 2013 was $825. A notice of the commission's licensing decision is received within 45 days. You will get your official license once you provide proof of financial responsibility through insurance or a bond.

To download this form FMC-18 from Federal Maritime Commission, click the link below.

http://www.fmc.gov/assets/1/Page/Application%20for%20a%20License%20as%20an%20Ocean%20Transportation%20Intermediary.pdf

TRUCKING FREIGHT FORWARDERS

It is beneficial to have some experience with a truck broker or freight forwarder but isn't necessary to get a license. The application is Form OP-1(FF) and can be completed online or by mail. After paying the $300 filing fee, you will get an FF number that you need to use in all future transactions with the FMCSA.

Here is the link to Federal Motor Carrier Safety Administration (FMCSA) site where you can fill the form OP-1(FF) online.

https://www.fmcsa.dot.gov/registration/op-1-ff-application-freight-forwarder-authority

You should also apply for cargo insurance as soon as possible in the amount of $5,000 property loss or damage for a single vehicle and $10,000 for any damage at one time or place. You will also need to apply a Form BOC-3 with the FMCSA where you need to mention each state that you plan to do business in and designate a person or company that will receive legal service for you.

Here is the link to BOC-3 from FMCSA site.

 https://www.fmcsa.dot.gov/registration/form-boc-3-designation-agents-service-process

AIRFREIGHT FREIGHT FORWARDERS

All airlines belong to the International Air Transport Association. Both cargo and freight airlines maintain administrative control of the industry by membership. If you don't take the IATA-provided courses, then you won't be able to access the forms data or electronic systems necessary to perform in this industry.

Therefore, you need to take the online course; the IATA Cargo Introductory Course. The course is $320 and requires 160 to 200 hours to complete. The course covers waybills, IATA operations manuals, the operation of freight forwarders and airline cargo units and cargo operations. There is a 3.5-hour examination offered by the IATA four times a year in March, June, September and December.

Here is the link to IATA site for Cargo Industry Course Registration.

http://www.iata.org/training/courses/Pages/cargo-introductory-tcgp11.aspx

INTERMODAL FREIGHT

This involves freight that is moved by more than one type of transportation. It is often placed on a truck first, but it may be loaded onto a ship, plane or rail car at some point. Intermodal freight has no individual license.

You don't need a railroad license since the receiving railroad arranges for rail transportation for all freight that is delivered to a railhead. However, for intermodal freight, a freight forwarder may need an FMCSA license along with an ocean transportation intermediary license if the shipment requires ocean shipping or an IATA certification if it is transported by air.

Knowing these types of requirements and the various responsibilities of a freight forwarder, many then have the question of whether or not just anyone can be a freight forwarder. Let's answer that question.

CAN ANYONE BECOME A FREIGHT FORWARDER?

The short answer is "yes," anyone can be a freight forwarder. Often all it takes to get started is an internet connection and a phone. However, this doesn't mean it is a simple and easy process. In order to be taken seriously by importer and exporters, you will need to have some qualifications and experience.

It is sometimes a good idea to get some training and expertise working in the sales department of a cargo management companies. This will help you learn how freight forwarding and the international shipping industry works, so you have a better perspective when you decide to go into business for yourself.

Remember how I got started? I worked as a document clerk, where my main job was to make copies, and organize files at first. We all have to get started somewhere.

Someone wants to know you have the knowledge and connections necessary for a smooth transaction before they're willing to hire you. So before you decide freight forwarding is right for you, let's consider whether or not you're suited to the job.

ARE YOU READY TO BE IN FREIGHT FORWARDING BUSINESS

Since freight forwarding is generally done in an office setting it is important that you have some everyday clerical experience. It also requires you to have communication skills, numeracy and ability to multi-task on several projects at the same time.

It is unlikely that you will work a typical 9 to 5 schedule with freight forwarding, so be prepared to work all hours. This is especially true when you have customers with tight delivery deadlines or when you simply need to contact people in different time zones and countries.

When it comes to a knowledge of the industry, a successful freight forwarder needs a broad range of abilities and skills. Freight forwarding is a complex market that has a number of different practices and regulations.

Most of your knowledge is theoretical and comes from studies; but can also involve international trade law, economics, finance or business. You will also need practical experience within the freight forwarding business or something similar.

The more awareness you have of overseas markets, shipping methods, insurance, paperwork, cargo, and customs procedures the better suited you will be for the job. Being able to comply with regulations is essential and knowing how to transport dangerous goods may even be required.

One word of advice for anyone reading this book, if you are set to start in this line of business, I am sure you understand you have to go through some training and licensing procedure first. But when you start, my advice is to start local, don't get into any international freight deals at first. Try and do only local (Within the US) freight forwarding.

This will give you a good head start, and you will learn the ropes fast. Once you are comfortable with the process, then move on to bigger and more complicated freights.

You will also need to build up a broad range of contacts when starting your company or attracting new business. This means you need to have a friendly disposition, patience and the ability to sell yourself to other companies and clients.

You should already have an idea of sectors or specific companies that you want to target as potential customers, so it is a good idea to have someone to go to for informal advice within the freight forwarding trade to start your company and get assistance as your business grows.

While English is the common language within international trade communities, you will have a head start over the competition if you can speak other languages. Linguistic abilities will allow you to add a personal touch when working closely with clients, customs departments, and shippers.

You also want to be prepared to travel occasionally, whether it be to your local airport or another country.

Now that you know what it takes to be a freight forwarder, you have a good idea if it is the type of business you want to start. If you still want to move forward then keep reading; next, we're going to look at what it takes to become a freight forwarder.

STEPS TO BECOME A FREIGHT FORWARDER

IF YOU are going to start a freight forwarding business, there are several questions you need to ask yourself, so you know where you need to start and what you need to address to be prepared to start your business.

Ask yourself the following questions:

✧ How extensive is your knowledge of transportation and cargo transport?

✧ How are your communication and negotiating skills?

✧ Are you comfortable working with a variety of people?

✧ If needed, do you have the drive and time required to get additional training?

✧ Do you prefer work as an independent contractor or with an established company?

- Do you want to focus on domestic shipments, international shipments or both?

Your answer to these questions as well as looking at the list of primary responsibilities below will help you to determine what you need to learn to get your business off to a good start.

- Advising clients on shipping and cargo requirements.

- Contacting carriers to find available transport options.

- Negotiating rates with both carriers and clients.

- Completing the necessary paperwork for all shipments.

- Searching for and attracting new clients.

- Attending related trade shows and transportation conferences to stay up to date.

- Doing research and staying informed about any new industry developments that impact you or your potential clients.

If you are entirely new to the freight forwarding business, you will need to start with the basics. In my opinion, there are two ways to get started in this business. First, you can start like I did, get a job doing anything at a freight forwarding business. Second, you can enroll yourself in some type freight forwarder course.

But remember, regardless how much education you get on this subject, some hands-on training will always go a long way. The first step is to understand the freight industry and what you need to get your business started.

UNDERSTANDING THE FREIGHT INDUSTRY

The first step before you even start to think about setting up your company is to have an understanding of how the freight industry works. Talk to people who are already involved in freight forwarding and have them explain the market segments to you.

They may even be able to offer you advice on setting up your business. If you don't know of anyone you can contact, you can also talk with your local chamber of commerce who can give you some advice on setting up your company.

GETTING STARTED

If you have no background or experience in the freight industry, it is highly recommended that you take a training course before starting your business. There are plenty of affordable training course options available. In addition to these training courses there are several legal documents you need to prepare.

Through the Federal Motor Carrier Safety Administration (FMCSA) you need to get a Broker's Authority.

Through a bank or bonding agency, you need to apply for a trust or surety bond in the amount of $10,000.

You need to apply as a Process Agent through the FMCSA which will give you authority to accept legal documents on behalf of clients.

A United States Department of Transportation (USDOT) number is needed, and you can also get this through the FMCSA.

Much of the freight industry today is managed over the internet. There are a number of freight matching websites that give you a list of carriers to match with the needs of a shipper.

These websites often require annual membership fees, but will often make up for the cost in terms of completed jobs and the amount of time you save.

Here are few of them you can take a look at:

http://cargomatchmaker.com

https://www.comfreight.com

https://truckstop.com

https://www.cargopedia.net

SETTING UP YOUR COMPANY

When setting up your company, the most important thing is to make sure you have all the paperwork in place. In this case, it is a good idea to have a professional help and if possible even hire a lawyer to make sure that all legal aspects of your company are covered.

You also want to make sure your contracts are written in such a way that will make each job clear and protect your rights. Otherwise, you will be facing a lot of legal issues later.

3 MUST DO'S

Getting started with a freight forwarding business is relatively easy, as long as you you take a step by step approcah, and get the necessary training. However, I've learned from experience and from talking to others in the industry that there are three specific things you need to do to get your business off to a good start.

NAME YOUR BUSINESS

You need to get customers to distinguish your service from others in the same industry. This means you are going to need a business name; and not just any name. You want a short name that is easy to remember while also being catchy.

You need to make sure the name you choose isn't being used by any other company. If you want to know about business names you need to contact the Patent and Trade Mark Office.

One good way to search is by searching the name you picked on Google to see if anyone else is using it for the same purpose. My advice is if you find a good name, go ahead and buy the domain name of the name you just picked, this way in future if you ever want to grow, you can have a website under that name.

You can go to Godaddy.com or name.com or any other domain name seller's site and just type the name you picked; they will tell you if that name is available for purchase with.com or .net. Typically most domain names cost around $10/year which in my opinion is a great investment.

LICENSE YOUR BUSINESS

All businesses need proper licenses to operate. Remember these licenses are different from what I spoke about earlier about permits and licenses from few federal agencies. These are the licenses you will need to operate as a business in your local city, county and state. This shows that you are running a legal business. However, before you are allowed to license a business, you need to determine a structure for your business. If you know an accountant or an attorney, ask them to file a legal business entity (Like an LLC, S Corp or LLP) on your behalf, this way you are legally protected from most business liabilities.

You can also go on websites like leaglzoom.com and have them draw up the document for less than what an attorney would charge you to do the same.

Once you file you file the article to incorporate your business, next step is to get an accountant or CPA to file and obtain an EIN(Employer's Identification Number) from IRS. This is similar to social security number but for business. Once you have these two documents, you can then open a commercial bank account at any local bank.

Next step would be to go to your local city office and find out what type of business and regulatory licenses you are required to have. It should take a day or two to get your licenses and permits in place, and then you are finally and officially in business.

Once you have a business license and a trademark name, customers will trust your products and be more likely to buy them.

COMPETITIVE ANALYSIS

This is key to having a successful business. When you have a competitive analysis, you know your business's current position within the freight forwarding industry in your area.

The competitive analysis allows you to get the information you need on your competitors, market share, market strategies, growth and other important factors. When you have all this information, you will be able to change or improve your business in key areas so you can increase profits and sales.

Here is a simple way you can do a competitive analysis. On a piece of paper write down the following:

1. Number of local competitors you have
2. What is their niche/market they service
3. Who they cater to
4. What is their pricing strategy

Once you have that list, take a look and see where you would fit in that list, how can you stand out from the crowd, what can you do differently that would make customers pay attention to your products.

In my business experience, I believe there are three ways you can always stand above the crowd. I always have tried to stand above the crowd by trying of these three strategies.

1. By providing superior service than my competitors provide
2. By offering 100% customer satisfaction guarantee
3. By creative pricing strategy

START UP COSTS

The first decision you need to make that will influence your startup costs is whether you plan to work from home or lease an office space. Obviously, if you choose to work from home it will reduce your start-up costs; but you will need to give careful consideration to how you are going to arrange your home office.

Leasing an office will cost you more, but it will also give you a good first impression when trying to find new customers and will allow you to separate your work life from your home life.

You will also need a reliable internet connection since this is your primary source of connection to deal with customers throughout the world.

You'll want to invest some money into well-designed stationery since this will help give a good first impression to your clients. Consider brochures and other marketing materials, all of which will vary in price based on the quality and color design you choose to go with.

To serve your local market, you need to have reliable transportation to nearby manufacturers. This allows you to oversee packaging, loading, and unloading of any imported or exported cargo.

You also need to consider your operating expenses. This can include advertising and promotional costs; insurance including employer's liability, public liability, a freight forwarder's liability policy and possibly professional indemnity insurance; and utility costs such as electricity, heating, and telephone. You also need to obtain a few professional Freight forwarder association memberships (FIATA), so it is easier for you to link with others and get referrals.

Lastly, you also want to make sure you have some cash reserves or an adequate bank facility since customers are going to expect you to have a level of credit. Some companies may also choose to get credit insurance. The need for firm credit control is something that can't be underestimated in the freight industry.

BUSINESS PLAN

Any new business needs a well-written business plan. For someone who's never written a business plan before, can be an intimidating process. Intimidating doesn't mean impossible; you can learn how to draft a freight forwarding business plan on your own.

Basically you are writing a business plan that describes where your business is headed and how you plan to achieve your goals. Throughout the startup process, you will be using your business plan to help guide you through decision making and strategic planning. So take the time to write a great business plan before you move on to the next step of starting your business.

FORMAL TRAINING

In general, basic freight forwarding isn't going to require any formal training or qualifications, but industry knowledge is both desirable and recommended.

However, if your freight forwarding business is complex; for example, if you are going to involve yourself in the handling of hazardous materials then

IATA regulations may require additional qualifications of yourself or one of your employees.

Within the freight industry, there are a wide range of training options available. Even if you have experience, you may find some courses will even help you fill in some gaps of your current freight knowledge. Consider some of the online courses available and what they may be able to teach you.

❖ The basics of sea freight.

❖ Introduction to air cargo. This is an IATA-approved course and in order to get approved you need to provide evidence that you employ at least two full-time employees with either the IATA approved course or FIATA Introductory Diploma.

❖ Customs procedures.

❖ The Multimodal Freight Training Program (MFT) Levels 1 and 2 that covers export documentation, international contracts, customs procedures and carriage of dangerous goods.

❖ Customer service for the freight industry will help you develop communication skills.

❖ Aviation security training.

❖ Dangerous goods training courses.

It is easy to see that there is no shortage of things you can learn to improve your business. However, this area is overshadowed by a number of legal issues you need to undertake to properly run your freight forwarding business.

LEGAL FACTORS IN STARTING A FREIGHT FORWARDING BUSINESS

THE government is highly particular about who is and isn't allowed to take part in freight forwarding services. This means that to start a freight forwarding business, you first need to register your business and obtain the appropriate licensing. Licenses need to be obtained on the basis of the country you are operation in and for the mode of transportation that your company is going to offer.

For example, within the United States, you will need to get licenses from multiple government agencies to ship by air, land, and sea. To find specifics on other countries you should contact the National Customs Brokers and Forwarders Association of America or other similar trade organizations to get information on regulations that apply to your business.

Here are the two websites that can tell you exactly what type of licenses and permits you will need based on your location and type of freight forwarding you are looking to do.

http://fiata.com

http://www.ncbfaa.org

FREIGHT FORWARDER LICENSE

Any trucking freight forwarder needs to be registered with the Federal Motor Carrier Safety Administration (FMCSA) in order to legally operate within the United States. This is the first step in becoming a licensed freight forwarder so you should get yourself acquainted with the FMCSA registration procedure.

Here is the FMCSA site where you can go and register.

https://www.fmcsa.dot.gov

The FMCSA is responsible for monitoring and ensuring the compliance of all motor carrier safety and commercial regulations. Companies may be subject to registration requirements for both safety and commercial regulations. Companies that are subject to the safety requirements will also need to get a USDOT Number.

The FMCSA registration process requires that companies define the type of Motor Carrier, Broker, Intermodal Equipment Provider (IEP), Cargo Tank Facility, Shipper and/or Freight Forwarder business operation they plan on establishing. The Agency is also responsible for administering the Federal Motor Carrier Safety Regulations (FMCSR) and Hazardous Materials Regulations (HMR) that govern interstate commercial trucking and bus industries.

The determination for this is based on self-classification of a company's proposed business operation based on criteria including cargo, operation and company type.

STEPS FOR FMCSA REGISTRATION

First, you need to determine FMCSA registration needs and requirements. This would be for a USDOT Number and Hazardous Materials Safety Permit Registration as well as Operating Authority or MC Number.

Companies that operate commercial vehicles transporting passengers or hauling cargo within interstate commerce need to register with the FMCSA and have a USDOT Number. Also, commercial interstate hazardous materials carriers who haul types and quantities need to have a safety permit and register for a USDOT (United States Department of Transportation) Number.

A USDOT Number is a unique identifier that helps in collecting and monitoring a company's safety information for audits, compliance reviews, crash investigations, and inspections.

You are required to get a USDOT number if you have a vehicle that is used to transport the types and quantities of hazardous materials requiring a safety permit. You are also required to get a USDOT number if you have a vehicle that has a gross vehicle weight rating or gross combination weight rating of 10,001 pounds or more.

Also if a vehicle is designed or used to transport more than eight passengers including the driver for compensation (commercial passenger van). As well as a vehicle that is designed or used to transport more than fifteen passengers including the driver and is not used to transport for the purpose of compensation.

Interstate commerce is defined as a trade, traffic or transportation in the United States:

➢ Between a place in a State and a place outside of that State or a place outside of the United States.

➢ Between two places within a State through another State or a place outside of the United States.

➢ Between two places within a State as a part of trade, traffic or transportation beginning or ending outside the State or the United States.

You are required to obtain a USDOT Number by the FMCSA and to comply with all Federal Regulations. It is the responsibility of drivers and motor carrier operators to know and comply with all Federal Motor Carrier Safety Regulations.

There are two types of companies that are required to have an Interstate Operating Authority or MC Number along with a USDOT Number.

1. Companies that transport passengers in interstate commerce.

2. Companies that transport federally-regulated commodities owned by others or those who arrange for their transport.

The FMCSA operating authority is often defined as an "MC," "FF," or "MX" Number based on the authority they grant. Unlike the application process for the USDOT Number, a company may need to get multiple operating authorities to support business operations. Operating Authority determines the type of operation a business can run and the cargo it will be able to carry.

Who Doesn't Need Operating Authority?

Operating authority also determines the level of financial responsibility and insurance a business needs to maintain. A carrier isn't required to have Operating Authority if they fit one of the three categories below:

1. Private carriers or those who transport their own cargo.

2. "For-hire" carriers that only haul exempt commodities, cargo that isn't federally regulated.

3. Carriers that operate only within a federally designated "commercial zone" that is exempt from interstate authority rules. For example, this would be a geographic territory that includes multiple states bordering on a major metropolitan city.

Types of Authority

The types of Operating Authority you request will determine the type and level of insurance the FMCSA requires. This means you should carefully choose only the types of Operating Authority that are relevant to your freight forwarding business.

You can't get a refund on application fees paid to the FMCSA. The following are the types of Interstate Operating Authority you can apply for:

➢ Motor Carrier of Property (except Household Goods)

➢ Motor Carrier of Household Goods (Moving Companies)

- Broker of Property (except Household Goods)

- Broker of Household Goods

- The United States based Enterprise Carrier of International Cargo (except Household Goods)

- The United States based Enterprise Carrier of International Household Goods

- Freight Forwarder Authority

- Motor Passenger Carrier Authority

- Non-North America-Domiciled Motor Carriers

- Mexico-based Carriers for Motor Carrier Authority to Operate Beyond U.S. Municipalities and Commercial Zones on the U.S.-Mexico Border

- Mexican Certificate of Registration for Foreign Motor Carriers and Foreign Motor Private Carriers

Filing Fees

It costs $300.00 to file for Operating Authority. You need to submit separate fees for each kind of authority you want to get.

Applying for Operating Authority

For a first-time applicant that hasn't registered with FMCSA and those who don't have a USDOT number, you need to apply through the Unified Registration System. If you already have a USDOT number or you are applying for additional authority, you can do it online.

New applications will often take 20-25 days unless they need further review, in which case it can take up to 8 weeks or even more. For an existing carrier, applications can take 45-60 days for approval.

The second step is to complete your FMCSA application process. To do this, you need to have specific insurance and legal process agent documents on file with the FMCSA. The required filings will vary depending on the registrations involved. Consider the following table showing insurance requirements.

Form	Description	Authorities Filing
BMC-91 or BMC-91X	Public liability insurance	Motor Carrier Freight Forwarder

BMC-34 or BMC-83	Cargo insurance - $5,000 per vehicle $10,000 per occurrence	Household Goods Motor Carrier Household Goods Freight Forwarder
BMC-84 or BMC-85	Surety Bond amount is $75,000 Trust Fund Agreement amount is $75,000	Freight Forwarder Broker of Freight
BOC-3	Service of Process Agents	All Authorities
MCS-90	Endorsement for Motor Carrier Policies of Insurance for Public Liability	Hazmat Safety Permit Carriers

How to File

Applicants need to contact their agents to request the filing of the required forms as soon as they get their designated docket number. Filings need to be received within 90 days of the FMCSA publishing public notice of intention to register an applicant.

The third step is to determine individual state notification and registration requirements.

The fourth step is to start the New Entrant Safety Assurance Program. This program affects the US and Canada based motor carriers. It is for a motor carrier not domiciled in Mexico that is applying for a US Department of Transportation ID number to start operations in interstate commerce.

A New Entrant needs to follow the following guidelines:

✓ Operate safely

✓ Maintain up-to-date records

✓ Conduct periodic inspections and perform maintenance on CMVs

✓ Pass the safety audit

A New Entrant will be monitored for an initial 18-month period. During this time the FMCSA will do three things:

1. Conduct a Safety Audit on the New Entrant

2. Monitor safety performance through roadside inspections

3. If safe, grant permanent authority

Safety Audits and Compliance Reviews

This is done by a certified US Federal Safety Investigator, State or Provincial Enforcement Office and the motor carrier which can include the manager, driver, mechanics or other staff.

The safety audit or compliance review is done within 12 months of starting business operations. It will happen again at any time that the FMCSA notices a problem on safety data.

The process will take place at the principal place of business.

A New Entrant will automatically fail their safety audit for violations related to the following:

Alcohol and Drug Violations:

➤ No alcohol and/or drug testing program

➤ No random alcohol and/or drug testing program

➤ Using a driver who refused a required test

➤ Using a driver, the company known has a blood alcohol of 0.04 or greater

➤ Using a driver who failed to complete required follow-up procedures after a positive test

Driver Violations:

➤ Using a driver without a valid CDL

➤ Using a driver who is disqualified

➤ Using a driver who has a revoked, suspended or canceled CDL

➤ <u>Using a medically unqualified driver</u>

Operations Violations:

➤ Operating a vehicle without the required level of insurance

➤ Failing to require hours-of-service records of drivers

Repairs and Inspections Violations:

➢ Operating an Out-of-Service vehicle due to safety deficiencies before appropriate repairs are made

➢ Not performing any OOS repairs based on driver-vehicle inspection reports

➢ Operation a CMV that isn't periodically inspected

If the safety audit is passed, the FMCSA will continue to monitor for safety compliance and performance. If the safety audit is failed, New Entrants need to satisfactorily implement corrective actions.

The fifth step is to get your permanent USDOT registration.

The sixth and final step is to maintain and update your USDOT Number and Operating Authority information as needed.

Freight forwarders often apply with form OP-1 (FF). This will get your Operating Authority number or FF number. This authority allows you to work across states. There are two possibilities for freight forwarding: property or household goods. If you want to cover both, then you need to apply for and pay the fee for both.

RECEIVING YOUR FF NUMBER

Once your application gets approved by the FMCSA, you will be issued an FF number in the form of a grant letter. Your approval will also be posted within the FMCSA Register. Anyone who disagrees with the registration can file a protest within 10 days. After this, your registration is secured.

Even though you have an FF number, you aren't ready to start business operations just yet.

Your FF number allows you to purchase the appropriate insurance, obtain your $75,000 freight broker bond or trust fund and designate processing agents if you want them. We'll discuss insurance further in a moment.

FREIGHT BROKER BOND

Freight forwarders are also required to post a security of $75,000 which guarantees legal compliance. This is often done in the form of a freight broker bond or a trust fund. Since trust funds are often more expensive and have more complications for freight forwarders;

most choose freight broker bonds in order to fulfill this part of the FMCSA requirement.

A freight broker bond is similar to a three-party contract. The freight forwarding business is the principal, the obligee is the FMCSA, and the surety is the one doing the bonding. The bond acts as an extra line of credit for your freight forwarding business. The purpose of it is to safeguard the interests of the public by guaranteeing that you comply with all rules and regulations.

While $75,000 seem like a high amount, just remember that you don't have to pay the whole amount in order to get your bond. Rather a surety bond cost will only be a small percentage of this, known as a bond premium. They typically range from 1 to 15 percent of the bond amount.

INSURANCE REQUIREMENT

When it comes to starting a small business like freight forwarding, there are a number of insurances involved. Without having adequate insurance coverage at the start of your business, you will be putting your company, employees and even your own assets at risk. You need the right level of liability coverage to protect yourself from the consequences of any lost or damaged shipments.

Other insurance is based on what type of freight you move and your methods of transportation. For example, if you are transporting by boat you may want to consider purchasing marine insurance.

This is specially designed to protect your company from cargo that is damaged or lost in international shipping. Let's first look at the reasons why you should get insurance for your freight forwarding business.

THE IMPORTANCE OF INSURANCE

As a freight forwarder, you are being entrusted with another's cargo. This makes you legally responsible for taking all the necessary steps to protect and preserve the cargo.

This means you become liable to the owner of the cargo for any damage or loss. As a forwarder, you are legally allowed to limit how much you are liable for, but these trading conditions need to be agreed to in advance.

When it comes to damaged or lost goods, it is possible that someone was negligent during the transportation process. If negligence is proven then the owner of the cargo is likely to demand compensation.

Even if the damage or loss isn't your fault, if it was caused by someone that you are responsible for such as a subcontractor then you are just as liable as the negligent person.

Freight forwarding is about a lot more than only handling cargo. A good portion of your business also involves using and providing information. A freight forwarder needs to know the following:

➢ When a method of transport is due to leave

➢ The import regulations of countries

➢ Current rate of duty for particular products

As a freight forwarder if you get any of this information wrong and a client is relying on you for accuracy you can still be liable. In the event of such mistakes, you can use trading conditions to limit the amount of compensation you are liable for.

You can have insurance to help cover any compensation you may end up being liable for. Let's consider the types of insurance a freight forwarder can and should consider.

TYPES OF INSURANCE

Two important types of insurance for freight forwarders to consider is a liability and marine insurance. As with any other small business, freight forwarders need public liability insurance and employer's liability insurance if you plan to have additional staff. It is also a good idea to have insurance for any premises (like a warehouse or something similar) you own and the contents they contain.

LIABILITY INSURANCE

This is the most important insurance that all freight forwarders should and need to have. This protects you from the types of compensation claims that we've discussed above in why you should have insurance.

You can find a wide range of liability insurance policies through a range of brokers. Although it is best that freight forwarders get their insurance through a specialist insurance broker that has experience with the relevant insurance policies based on the freight industry. Liability insurance won't protect the cargo itself since this is often the responsibility of the buyer or seller.

MARINE INSURANCE

This insurance will cover the loss or damage of any goods that are being transported internationally. Despite their name, marine insurance will also cover air, road, and rail transport methods.

Since freight forwarders and carriers are entitled to placing a limit on their liability, owners of cargo that don't insure the goods during international transport are only entitled to a fraction of the real value of the cargo. Most freight forwarders choose to get this type of insurance because it can provide added value to their services when requested by customers.

Now that we've taken a look at the requirements for starting a freight forwarding business let's take a look at your options for getting started.

STARTING A FREIGHT FORWARDING BUSINESS

AFTER all this talk of the requirements, insurance and legal issues of starting a freight forwarding business you are likely feeling a little overwhelmed. I won't lie to you, it is a lot of work to start a freight forwarding business; but no more so than most small businesses. If you are driven and don't mind a little work, it isn't that difficult to start a freight forwarding business.

However, if all this work still makes you second guess starting into this line of work the good news is that there are two options for making it easier starting a freight forwarding business.

PURCHASING A FREIGHT FORWARDING BUSINESS

The first option you have instead of starting your own freight forwarding business from scratch is to consider buying an existing freight forwarding business.

Although this isn't to say this option is completely hassle-free. When it comes to buying a business, there are no reliable shortcuts.

If you choose to go this route your first step should be to contact a business broker. While you can certainly buy a freight forwarding business on your own; you will save both time and money by using a reputable broker with experience in the freight industry. Then once you buy a company, you will have an already established business without all the hassle of starting your own freight forwarding business from the ground up and all the hassles that go with it.

FRANCHISE

Buying a pre-existing freight forwarding business can be a good option, but not everyone is going to be able to afford this option. So another option you can consider is to franchise your freight forwarding business. This option gives you an improved chance of becoming a successful business owner.

Before you choose to start your own freight forwarding business, it is best to look into the franchising option and whether or not it can help you on your business journey. With this option, you'll still be starting your own business, but you'll be getting the necessary support you need from an established company.

This will reduce your costs and will give you a built-in support system if you need help along the way. Remember, franchise businesses always have a better chance of success than non-franchise ones.

Here are 4 top franchised freight businesses according to Entrepreneur magazine, follow the link to see how much they cost and how to contact them.

https://www.entrepreneur.com/franchises/category/bsship

RUNNING A FREIGHT FORWARDING BUSINESS

ONCE you've started your freight forwarding business, you need to be prepared for some competition. It is important to do some research on who your biggest competitors are and what type of competition you can expect in the freight forwarding business so you can overcome it.

Obviously, your main source of competition is going to come from other freight forwarders whether they are small businesses or multinational corporations. The level of threat they present to your business will depend on the type of business you want to concentrate on and the types of customers you aim to attract.

A small business or a single individual freight forwarder may specialize in a specific region or on an individual industry. It isn't uncommon for a small business or individual to serve a unique niche for years with little to no competition. It may be possible to easily compete with these companies by offering better skills, price, and services; by attempting to meet the increasingly sophisticated needs of customers, you can easily have a leg up on the competition.

Large multinational freight forwarding companies have many advantages over their competition. Some of these companies even have their own ships and haulers, they may handle enough freight that they have regular space reserved on shipping lines, and many often have branches located in different countries.

Manufacturers who want an integrated service prefer these companies because of their ability to offer supply chain management covering everything from the supply of components and materials to the distribution of completed goods.

Often the best way to compete with these larger corporations is to do everything you can to smoothly and efficiently run your business. Let's look at some ways you can do this.

TRADING CONDITIONS AND LIMITING LIABILITY

All businesses are subject to a number of statutory regulations regarding employment law, health and safety, public liability and accounting standards. In addition to these general regulations, freight forwarders also have specific legal issues that affect them and their customers.

It is easy to see where things can go wrong. You are dealing with a journey of several thousand miles that probably involves more than a single mode of transport. However, before this happens a sale and contract need to be agreed upon between the seller and buyer of the goods; then a freight forwarder is needed. The nature of this initial contract will often directly influence the details of the contract between a freight forwarder and their client who is either the seller or buyer of the cargo.

TRADING CONDITIONS

For the client to completely understand and for both parties to agree on the responsibilities of the transportation process; the freight forwarder needs to make the client aware of trading conditions. This needs to be the first thing done before any details of the contract are discussed and agreed upon. This will come at the stage of presenting a quote.

Discussing trading conditions will establish the circumstances under which the freight forwarder is providing services and helps to limit the freight forwarders liability should a claim be filed against them. Failing to do this can leave a freight forwarder with unlimited liability and a costly mistake if something goes wrong.

In addition, when you go over trading conditions you will be ensuring the following:

➢ the clients know their goods aren't insured automatically

➢ safeguards the freight forwarder to ensure they are paid upon completion of the job

➢ protects the freight forwarder should the client fail to completely disclose the contents of a shipment

Even when limiting liability, a freight forwarder still needs to take some responsibility in the event of lost or damaged cargo.

MANAGING THE RISKS

Freight forwarders are responsible for goods and documents owned by third parties that can often be of high value. This means that risk management is an important part of running a successful freight forwarding business.

Insurance policies can only cover some of the risks and limit liability to a degree. You can easily invalidate all of these benefits by having carelessness or ignorance. There are also some risks that aren't insurable such as losses caused by acts of terrorism. It is impossible to completely eliminate all risks, but through proper training and good business practices, a freight forwarder can minimize these risks to an acceptable level. As a result, this will reduce the chance of unwanted claims that can impact the profits of your business.

This is why the first step above of bringing trading conditions to the attention of the clients before a contract is concluded is important. If you don't do this, it can prejudice insurance coverage and invalidate limited liability protections. Then there are other areas of a freight forwarding business where you need to have clear procedures that are understood by all your employees.

These areas include the following:

➢ Written instructions from clients

➢ Steps regarding the issue and release of documents

➢ Written contracts when managing or dealing with subcontractors

➢ Instructions for handling dangerous goods

➢ Steps for cargo security

➢ Procedures for insurance claims

This also brings us to an important area: how to determine when you are transporting dangerous goods. One thing I was truly surprised with is just how many dangerous (hazardous) goods are hidden in cargo that otherwise seemed normal. Let's learn how you can identify hidden dangerous goods.

HIDDEN DANGEROUS (HAZARDOUS) GOODS

There is no shortage of complex goods today that contain some substance or another than can be damaging to the environment or potentially harmful to human health. These commodities are often known as hidden dangerous goods.

A good example would be of batteries (especially the lithium-ion type batteries that can explode at high altitude) within the equipment. Another example would be for commodities containing magnetized material such as speakers.

It may not seem like much, but the transportation of goods like this present a challenge for even an experienced freight forwarder. Often it involves a discussion with the client who pretends their cargo isn't classified as hazardous material while carriers view the cargo as a safety risk. The most concerned carrier is air cargo transportation, but it can happen in other transportation modes as well.

While the client and carrier may have differing views, the freight forwarder is the one who faces all the negative impacts and uphill struggle of transporting these goods. With some careful approaches and necessary professional care you can often avoid this difficult and unpleasant discussion.

Consider an example. When shipping flashlights from the United States to the Middle East. Everything was going fine until the carrier refused to load the equipment. The reason was improper labeling from the shipper. This resulted in major additional cost for moving the freight back to the shipper to be re-labeled properly.

This issue could have been avoided had the freight forwarder made sure the shipment was ready and that the shipper was aware of what needed to be done to ship these hidden hazardous goods.

As a freight forwarder, you can't be expected to know all commodities and how they need to be classified, but there are some simple rules you can follow to avoid disputes with customers or at least make them easier to deal with.

The first thing a freight forwarder needs to insist on is to get the weight and dimension of the freight and also to request some classification details of the commodity or goods being shipped. This should be done before any proposal or booking. Always get specifics and never accept a general answer that doesn't adequately describe what the cargo is.

The second thing to do once you know what the cargo is to ask yourself if there is a chance that it could contain a hidden hazardous material. With some experience, you can easily answer nearly all of the cases that come your way.

If you know, there is hidden hazardous material, or if you aren't sure, then you simply need to ask for the MSDS (Material Safety Data Sheet). In general, if the goods being transported have an MSDS then it is highly probable that the goods are harmful to some extent. The MSDS will tell you just how hazardous the cargo is.

The third thing you want to do is to check the MSDS. You won't even have to read through the whole thing. Simply look at the Transportation and Storage section of the MSDS, and you will often find one or two sentences to give you all you need to know.

If the MSDS doesn't list any special requirements for transportation, then you are ready to proceed. If you find an abbreviation starting with UN and four digits, then you are going to have a little more work. This means the goods are hazardous and you are going to need to talk with a DGR (Dangerous Goods Regulations) specialist within your company and the carrier to work out transportation options.

If you do these three quick and simple things each time, then you can head off potential conflicts with customers, which makes it a better experience for all involved.

Now that you've likely started running your business let's consider a few things you can do to promote and expand your business into a thriving and profitable one.

PROMOTING YOUR BUSINESS

TO successfully promote your freight forwarding business, you need to understand who your customers are going to be. Your clients are going to often be one of three: exporters, importers or other freight forwarders. Your business may deal with haulers and other freight carriers operating between towns, regions, and countries.

You may also be contracted by foreign companies who want to arrange for the import of their freight from abroad. The way I have gotten many of these international contracts is through FIATA, by having our company name listed on their websites, anyone needed to find a freight forwarder in New Orleans area, contacted us. That is why I mentioned the importance of having memberships in these types of associations.

It is also possible that you can get long term contracts. Most of these are with manufacturers to oversee the regular movement of shipments from specific ports. Other manufacturers start a long term contract in order to consolidate service for smaller freight volumes.

Many smaller freight forwarding businesses often specialize in a specific type of freight or in the carriage of cargo between certain areas. It can be a good idea to consider channeling your knowledge into one of the following specialty areas:

➢ Companies within the sports and entertainment business often use freight forwarding as a way to arrange transports of concert sets, sports equipment, exhibitions and film sets.

➢ Importers of perishable goods often want to work with a single and reliable freight forwarder. They are looking for the transport of fresh fruit and vegetables, fish, and horticultural products along with refrigerated meat and other foods.

➢ Agricultural countries often require the movement of livestock.

➢ Medical and pharmaceutical supply companies want freight forwarders who are aware of the careful handling and special conditions needed.

- ➢ Heavy industries who manufacture components and assembles for industries such as aerospace, power generation and shipbuilding require specialized knowledge and expertise.

- ➢ Car and automotive parts manufacturers often require transport across international boundaries.

Once you understand your customer focus, you can start to look at promoting your business. Let's look at some ways you can do this.

HOW TO PROMOTE

The promotional efforts you use should be directed towards your target market. This will allow you to emphasize your ability and your special knowledge while allowing you to reduce costs for yourself and your client. Consider some good promotional options.

The first good place to start is the Yellow Pages (online yellow pages). While a display advertisement can be expensive, it gives you the advantage of promoting your business for an entire year. Many also offer you to include your listings online for a slightly higher cost.

Another good option is to approach the local chamber of commerce. Here you can meet with local business and start to build your reputation and business network. Most chambers have networking events, seminars, and training days that can help you get to know export documentation and overseas market while also developing contacts and potential clients.

You can also get your name out by advertising in various trade-related magazines. This means looking into business periodicals within your area or magazines that are focused on your specific sectors. Make sure you have a budget and design for your advertising planned in advance.

Put together a list of local manufacturers that includes addresses and contact names. This allows you to promote your business on a continuous basis through both mailings and personalized letters that make logistics managers aware of your freight forwarding services.

Lastly, a website is a key factor for freight forwarders and is a way for others to find you. However, you should also design it with the goal of attracting attention to you as well.

Since freight is an international industry, you want to make sure the most important parts of your website are translated into the most relevant languages. Clearly, display your phone number and international dialing code(For example, USA's dialing code is 1, whereas Indias's dialing code is 91) so people calling from abroad know how to reach you.

Also, make sure you register with the most popular directory websites, so you come up in online searches. A website also needs to be a showcase for all the services you have to offer.

3 KEYS TO A SUCCESSFUL AND PROFITABLE BUSINESS

The success of a freight forwarder depends on experience, skill level, and economic factors. However, there are a few key things you can do to ensure a successful and profitable business.

First, you need to master the art of negotiation. Most matches between a shipper and carrier start with a dollar amount that the shipper is willing to pay and a dollar amount that a carrier expects to receive. The job of the freight forwarder is to get the best match based on the cargo to price benefit your client. You also do this to pay yourself since you earn commission on the cargo you set up for your clients. After all, time is money.

You also need to keep up with current events. Economic conditions have a direct impact on the freight forwarding business. In particular, fuel prices will sometimes require you to negotiate for better prices and accept lower commissions at times.

Lastly, you want to stay ahead of problems. Carriers won't be on time all the time. Occasionally, accidents, weather or unforeseen occurrences will delay shipments and deliveries. Maintain contact with the shipper and the carrier. If a shipment is going to be late, inform your client. If a carrier is routinely late, find one that is more reliable. Clients won't work with you if your shipments are constantly late or often have damage.

3 STEPS TO SELLING YOUR SERVICES

When it comes to selling your services as a freight forwarder, the goal is to generate a result. Selling your services involves manipulating input to get the results you desire.

The sales process starts when promotion and marketing end. The sales lead and the cold calls are the inputs involved in the sales process. Let's take a quick look at the freight forwarding sales process. There are three steps you need to do.

The first step is to determine what you're selling. It is easy to answer that you sell freight or transportation, but neither of these are true for freight forwarders. While this is a part of what you do, you actually are offering so much more; organization, coordination, and consolidation of services. All of these are focused on the proper movement of a client's freight between two locations. This is what you need to focus on selling to clients.

The second step is to focus on how you sell yourself. The key is not to overwhelm prospective clients with information about your business and the services you offer. This is the wrong approach that certainly won't get to sales.

Rather you want to approach it from the point of view of what the customer wants. What kinds of transportation is the client going to use, how do they perceive the freight industry, what is their understanding of your services and what is the most important aspect to them. You find the answer to these by listening to the client and asking the right questions.

Selling freight forwarding services is much different from other items. You won't impress a client if you tell them you can ship items across international borders if this isn't something they need. Either do your homework about potential clients before making a cold call or start selling from the sales lead.

Lastly, you need to know when to stop the sell. This is possibly the easiest step. You will stop selling your services if one of two things happen. Either your prospective client will tell you to they aren't interested or they will place an order with you. Once you get an order, stop selling and focus on serving your client and meeting their needs so you can get repeat orders.

When it comes to promoting and selling your services, one thing you will find often is clients who want a price quote. Let's look at the elements that go into this so you can adequately quote a price for potential clients.

THE ELEMENTS OF A PRICE QUOTE

You will often get a client request for a price quote without much information other than locations. You need specific information to give an adequate price quote. International transportation is a very complicated process, and there are a number of activities involved that can influence the cost of transport.

If a client requests a rate from you, then it is recommended that you get some basic information, so you don't have to play tag with the client to clarify information. Let's look at the main elements of a price quote that you need to get to make your price calculation more accurate.

LOADING/UNLOADING ADDRESS

When it comes to the United States, Canada, and EU countries, you won't need any more than the name of a city/town and the post/ZIP code. However, for South East Asia or India, you are going to need the complete address, and you need to be precise.

TERMS OF DELIVERY

This is one of the most important and yet often forgotten elements of a price quote. This is where you need to focus on the terms of delivery. FOB, EXW, DAP are all great information to help you know what cost elements to include in your price quote.

GROSS WEIGHT AND PACKAGE DIMENSIONS

A lot of time you will only get the gross weight of a shipment. Maybe you'll also get the volume of the shipment. This often isn't enough, especially if you need an air freight quote. In air freight there are specific limitations on single unit dimensions and gross weight; these limitations will also vary based on the airplane.

Air freight also has different packaging from the typical cartons, so you need as accurate dimensions as possible. This will save you a lot of hassle and cost with cargo being placed on hold or rejected simply because it won't fit into the cargo bay of a plane or container.

DESCRIPTION OF GOODS

You are always going to run into customers that don't want to disclose what commodity they are having you transport. If a customer wants to keep the contents secrets, then they shouldn't be using a freight forwarder. Shipping lines and airlines have very specific rates for certain commodities. This is why it is best to know what you are shipping from the beginning.

INSURANCE

Most freight forwarders don't quote for insurance unless asked. Always ask for insurance terms, it might increase your cost, but it is worth it.

GOODS VALUE

This is related to the cost of cargo insurance. For some specific goods such as valuables then getting the goods, the value is important. It is also important to note that in some countries this is calculated in the customs bond, duties and taxes.

TERMS OF TRANSPORT

Some specific terms of transportation are necessary for some commodities. For example, if you are shipping vaccines then you have a narrow temperature range to maintain, so you don't destroy the vaccines. So be sure to ask clients about any special ways of transporting if there is a potential they will be different from normal transportation options. For example, you wouldn't ship vaccines by ocean freight since the containers have a high humidity environment with wide temperature ranges.

Using these guides can allow you to make clear and precise price quotes for potential clients. Lastly, let's consider what resources are available to you as a small business freight forwarder to help you as you continue to operate your business.

RESOURCES

As a small business freight forwarder, you often have more flexibility than a larger forwarding company. While it may seem like you lake the resources of a larger company, this often isn't the case. With a little design and planning, you can compensate for fewer resources. Let's consider what your options are.

BONDED WAREHOUSE

As you are probably aware of, the price of establishing and maintaining warehouse operations is high. Most warehouses come with a fixed cost, which means that whether you have traffic or not you are going to be spending these funds.

Consider instead outsourcing the activity to a company that operates a warehouse, and you can get a variable cost for your bonded warehouse. This way you will only be paying per shipment, allowing you to be flexible and competitive.

CUSTOMS BROKERAGE DEPARTMENT

So your customers have a steady and smooth customs brokerage you need to hire at least two customs brokers who know the procedures well and follow the daily changes in this area. You can easily see how this cost will add up when it comes to salaries, social and medical insurance, training, hardware and software along with other necessary equipment. Plus you never know how long an employee will stay with you.

Instead, save money by sub-contracting this activity to highly experienced customs brokers that you can easily use to process customers' orders. Again you will only be paying on a per shipment basis rather than an employee cost. This means the quality of your service also increases as long as you monitor and control the process.

SOFTWARE AND HARDWARE

CRM, OMS, ERP, etc. - the more the abbreviations, the higher licensing fees you pay. However, this is only if you are dependent on MS. When it comes to operating systems you have two choices, Ubuntu and Windows.

I suggest you avoid Microsoft products if you can. Ubuntu is a lighter system than MS systems. It also works better on older hardware and is very stable. Best of all Ubuntu is free and more secure since you don't have to pay for licenses. You only have to pay for installation and training if you aren't able to do it on your own.

So now I've told you the majority of everything you need to know. In closing, I want to leave you with some ideas on expanded your business so you can see where you can go from here.

HOW TO GROW YOUR BUSINESS

THE first goal of becoming a freight forwarder is to build up a client base. Once you have a working relationship with carriers and customers, you will want to expand your services. Consider the following ideas when you want to take your business to the next level:

➢ Hire additional brokers and start a freight forwarding agency.

➢ Ship additional commodities to expand your services.

➢ Start teaching freight forwarding classes.

➢ Purchase a fleet of trucks and start your own specialized shipping service.

Once you master and specialize one niche, venture into another and continue to grow that way.

Remember if you can master various niches, then you will always see less competition compare to most other general freight forwarding businesses. This way you will always enjoy a healthy and positive growth in your business.

LAST WORDS

REMEMBER, as I said, this industry will grow by around 6%-10% every year, and that growth can translate into many hundreds of new freight forwarding business.

The potential is unlimited, and by you entering this line of business, you will not be slicing the pie smaller, because the growth will need and require newcomers to take some of the extra load from the established freight forwarding businesses.

Another piece of advice I want to offer, if you want to start small, and have a little warehouse or even an empty garage, get started with Amazon FBA sellers.

Market yourself towards Amazon sellers. There are many Amazon FBA seller groups and sites you can find online or on Facebook, market yourself to them, and you will enjoy a great and comfortable start in your business.

Once you get your feet wet with Amazon FBA, then you can venture into bigger clients.

If you need to get in touch with me or have problem downloading any of the forms, you can email me at AllenTheFreightGuy@gmail.com

Good Luck!

GLOSSARY OF TERMS

TPP – Trans Pacific Partnership

TAP – Trans Atlantic partnership

FBA- Fulfilled by Amazon

NVOCC - Non-vessel operating common carrier

FMCSA - Federal Motor Carrier Safety Administration

IATA - International Air Transport Association

FIATA – International Federation of Freight Forwarders Associations

FMT - Multimodal Freight Training Program

USDOT - United States Department of Transportation

IEP - Intermodal Equipment Provider

FMCSR - Federal Motor Carrier Safety Regulations

HMR - Hazardous Materials Regulations

MSDS - Material Safety Data Sheet

DGR - Dangerous Goods Regulations

FOB – Free on Board

EXW – Ex Works

DAP- Delivered at place

FORMS AND LINKS

Application for a License as an Ocean Transportation Intermediary – Form FMC -18 from Federal Maritime Commission.

http://www.fmc.gov/resources/forms_and_applications.aspx

Here is the link to all insurance related forms from Federal Motor Carrier Safety Administration site.

https://www.fmcsa.dot.gov/registration/registration-forms#Process-Agent

Application for Designation Agents for Service Process from FMCSA site.

Form BOC-3

https://www.fmcsa.dot.gov/registration/form-boc-3-designation-agents-service-process

Form MCS -90 from FMCSA site

https://www.fmcsa.dot.gov/registration/form-mcs-90-endorsement-motor-carrier-policies-insurance-public-liability-under

Form BMC -85 from FMCS site

https://www.fmcsa.dot.gov/registration/form-bmc-85-broker%E2%80%99s-or-freight-forwarder%E2%80%99s-trust-fund-agreement-under-49-usc-13906-o-0

Form OP-1 (FF) from FMCSA site

https://www.fmcsa.dot.gov/registration/op-1-ff-application-freight-forwarder-authority

Here is the IATA link to all their freight forwarder training courses

http://www.iata.org/training/courses/Pages/cargo-introductory-tcgp11.aspx

Here is the FIATA site for all things related to freight forwarder, this site is a must visit for anyone looking to get started in this business.

http://fiata.com